Stock Car
Secrets

JIM FRANCIS

x1000r/min

CRABTREE PUBLISHING COMPANY
www.crabtreebooks.com

Crabtree Publishing Company

www.crabtreebooks.com

Coordinating editor
Chester Fisher

Series and project editor
Shoreline Publishing Group LLC

Author
Jim Francis

Project Manager
Kavita Lad (Q2AMEDIA)

Art direction
Rahul Dhiman (Q2AMEDIA)

Design
Tarang Saggar (Q2AMEDIA)

Cover Design
Ravijot Singh (Q2AMEDIA)

Photo research
Anasuya Acharya & Amit Tigga (Q2AMEDIA)

Manuscript development and photo research
assistance provided by Shoreline Publishing Group
LLC, Santa Barbara, California

Acknowledgments

The publishers would like to thanks the following
for permission to reproduce photographs:

AP Photo: Gene Blythe: page 23 (bottom right);
   Chuck Burton: pages 8-10, 12, 14; Eric Jamison:
   page 17; James P. Kerlin: page 5; Reinhold Matay:
   page 20; Wade Payne: page 7 (top); John Russell:
   pages 7 (bottom right), 13
Grey Villet/Time Life Pictures/Getty Images: page 4
Joe Robbins: cover, title page, pages 6, 11, 15, 16,
   18, 19, 21, 22, 23 (top left), 24-31

Cover: Race Crew works on Engine.

Title page: During a pit stop, jack man lifts the car.

Library and Archives Canada Cataloguing in Publication

Francis, Jim, 1963-
    Stock car secrets / Jim Francis.

(NASCAR)
Includes index.
ISBN 978-0-7787-3189-4 (bound).--ISBN 978-0-7787-3197-9 (pbk.)

    1. Stock cars (Automobiles)--Juvenile literature. I. Title. II. Series:
NASCAR (St. Catharines, Ont.)

GV1029.9.S74F733 2007   j629.228   C2007-907255-0

Library of Congress Cataloging-in-Publication Data

Francis, Jim, 1963-
    Stock car secrets / Jim Francis.
       p. cm. -- (NASCAR)
    Includes index.
    ISBN-13: 978-0-7787-3189-4 (rlb)
    ISBN-10: 0-7787-3188-X (rlb)
    ISBN-13: 978-0-7787-3197-9 (pb)
    ISBN-10: 0-7787-3197-9 (pb)
    1. Stock cars (Automobiles)--Juvenile literature. I. Title.
    TL236.28.F73 2008
    629.228--dc22
                                                        2007048442

Crabtree Publishing Company

Published in Canada
Crabtree Publishing
616 Welland Ave.
St. Catharines, ON
L2M 5V6

Published in the United States
Crabtree Publishing
PMB16A
350 Fifth Ave., Suite 3308
New York, NY 10118

Published in the United Kingdom
Crabtree Publishing
White Cross Mills
High Town, Lancaster
LA1 4XS

Published in Australia
Crabtree Publishing
386 Mt. Alexander Rd.
Ascot Vale (Melbourne)
VIC 3032

CONTENTS

Stock Car Secrets

Those NASCAR racecars look sort of familiar, don't they? Looks like they just pulled out of the family garage, right? Wrong! The cars used in NASCAR are some of the most high-tech racing machines in the world. Let's find out how they are made.

Made for Racing

In NASCAR, it's all about the cars. Fans watch those cars and cheer for their favorite drivers as the vehicles zoom around the track. The huge engines of the colorful cars rattle fans' eardrums, while the familiar colors and numbers let fans look for top drivers. Meanwhile, the drivers

A Sunday drive? No, the start of a race. But it was not unusual for early NASCAR drivers to use the family car on race weekends.

depend on the design of the cars to keep them from flying into the walls. Back in the pits, crew members track the performance of the engine and other parts. During all of this, NASCAR officials make sure that everyone is following the rules— and they catch the folks who aren't. All of this action surrounds every NASCAR racecar. But those cars don't just come out of a factory like the cars that you see on the streets of your town. NASCAR cars are specially designed for racing.

They use engines that are about twice as big as in passenger cars. But wait a minute—the "SC" in NASCAR stands for "**stock car**." A stock car is one that *does* come from a factory. It is the standard model sold by a carmaker to drivers around the country (or the world). So what's going on? The answer is that NASCAR races began using stock cars . . . but that changed pretty quickly.

The First "Stock" Cars

When NASCAR started in 1948, the drivers did use cars that had been made in a factory. In some cases, they drove their family cars right from home onto the racetrack. You can see in some old pictures that drivers used white tape to put numbers on the sides of these cars. In one race, fans might see a dozen or more different types of cars. Some were two-door, some four-door. Some had long, stretched-out hoods, while others were shorter and blunter. Even the drivers went their own way, wearing everything from full jumpsuits to jeans and T-shirts. However, since the goal of each driver was to go faster than the other guys, they soon tried to change, or "soup up," these stock cars to gain speed. To make sure that their races were fair, one of NASCAR's first rules was that cars had to be "stock." By keeping the changes that drivers made to a minimum, the races depended on the drivers, not the fancy cars. Many carmakers looked to these races as a way to promote their cars. Fans watching Chevrolets, Hudsons, and Fords on a weekend might decide to go buy one of those cars the next week. This meant that those makers wanted the cars to be as "stock" as possible. But again, that soon changed.

Stock Gets Slicker

By the late 1950s, as NASCAR got bigger and bigger, the cars became less and less "stock." The basic designs of the bodies were still similar to those sold by the carmakers. The engines, however, got much larger. Also, many more safety parts were added to the cars. Roll bars were added in 1952. Heavier parts were used around the wheels—springs, shocks, **axles**, etc.—to withstand the pounding. For many years, for instance, the windshields were still made of glass. NASCAR racers changed to a form of plastic, though, to protect the drivers. They removed more and more items that were needed on a passenger car, but not on a racecar. Finally, in the mid-1950s, drivers started using larger engines made just for racing, not for street use. The small block V-8, introduced in 1955, is called "one of the important changes in stock car history," by NASCAR.com. The move to "real" racing machines was on.

NASCAR driver Joe Weatherly shows off the homemade car number on his 1952 racecar— it's made with tape!

Built for Racing

By the 1980s, NASCAR cars were getting almost completely away from "stock." Race teams signed up with carmakers to supply them with engines and car parts. Those carmakers also chose which of their cars would serve as the models for the NASCAR vehicles. For example, Bill Elliott, the 1988 NASCAR champ, drove a Ford Thunderbird. Now, this was not an exact copy of the Thunderbirds driving around U.S. streets, but Bill's car did look like that Thunderbird, thus helping Ford sell more of them. That's how NASCAR vehicles were designed into the mid-2000s. Carmakers and NASCAR would agree on which car models would become NASCAR racers. Then the teams would make the cars based on those models, following a strict set of rules. However, as with everything in NASCAR over the years . . . that way of working changed, too.

The Car of Tomorrow

Beginning in 2008, all NASCAR racing teams will use the same body style and shape. Created by NASCAR after years of testing, the Car of Tomorrow (COT) will mean that all cars in every race will be nearly the exact same size and shape. That's a big change from the hodgepodge of early NASCAR races in which fans might see a dozen different body types. The reasons for the change included fairness, money, and safety. By having one body type for all teams, NASCAR has made it harder for teams to make cars that have an unfair advantage. Before the COT, teams might make a car slightly different to gain a little more speed. Also, having one body saves the teams money by letting them focus on engines only and not have to build a brand-new body shape each week. Finally, as we'll see later on, the COT made a few changes that will keep drivers safer during races . . . and during crashes.

Here's a good look at the basic NASCAR stock car of the early 2000s, before the Car of Tomorrow came into full use. The 18 and 15 cars are Chevrolets, while the 17 car is a Ford . . . but they're not "stock" anymore! They're built for racing.

> Notice the wing on the back of Jeff Gordon's Car of Tomorrow. Designers put it there to create a force that holds the car on the track.

Building a Stock Car

Now that NASCAR has set up the COT as the standard for its top-level Sprint Cup races, how do those cars make it to the racetrack? That's what this book is all about. We'll go step-by-step and watch as today's stock car is built. You'll see that it takes a big team of experts, and lots of technology, to get those cars ready to thrill fans. That's a big change from NASCAR's early days, when drivers would take regular cars and add a few parts to make them race-ready. Today, with millions of dollars on the line for drivers, that has all changed. However, even with all the newfangled technology, one thing remains the same. No matter what the car or how it gets built, the drivers of those cars have one goal— to win the race. Now let's look at how technology has changed how cars are built.

Drivers like Jeff Gordon can tell their teams how they want the rear wing adjusted to match their personal driving styles.

Framing the Car

NASCAR fans see the colorful bodies of their favorite cars, but they don't see the most important parts of those cars. Beneath all the stickers and paint is a steel cage that forms the car and keeps the driver safe.

The Skeleton of a Stock Car

The skeleton of a stock car is called the **chassis** (pronounced CHASS-ee). A car's chassis is made of steel tubes and forms the basic shape of the car. Over the years, the chassis of NASCAR vehicles has changed a lot, getting longer and sleeker and sturdier. New materials have also made it safer, but at the same time lighter, thus making it faster. Your family car has a chassis, too, with many of the same goals. However, knowing that NASCAR crashes happen at much higher speeds, the chassis of these cars are much, much stronger. The main section of the chassis is the center section, known as the "roll cage." This is made of the heaviest steel and is supposed to stay in one piece, uncrushed, during a crash. This cage protects the driver in almost every crash. Thanks to the roll cage, some drivers have walked away, dizzy but unhurt, after a crash. The rest of the car might break apart, but the roll cage stays together.

Here's a good look at the COT chassis. Notice the steel tubes that form the roll cage.

Computers at Work

One of the most important parts of making the COT is a computer. No, the designers don't play video games (though the drivers do...a lot of them think that it helps them on the track). Rather, the computers are used to create many different chassis designs. They are looking for just the right one. The computers can model tiny changes to the chassis and show how those changes might affect the speed or safety or cost of the car. Computer Aided Design (CAD) experts use different programs to create the chassis shape, including which types of steel tubes should be

A NASCAR official shows off the computer drawing that helped create the Car of Tomorrow. Notice the large purple section: that's the "firewall" between the engine compartment and the driver.

used in each section of the chassis. Tests can be run on the computer to simulate wind and air traveling over the car. And the computer can run crash tests to demonstrate the safety of each design. Computers also can help carmakers decide what materials to use or how engines will fit into the chassis.

This close-up photo shows how steel bars crisscross the interior of the roll cage. These bars and the metal floor protect the driver during a high-speed crash.

The Skeleton's Bones

Along with the roll cage, the basic chassis has two other main sections. The "front clip" supports the front axle and the engine. It is made of steel tubes and bars that are supposed to crumple in a high-speed crash. This absorbs the energy of the crash and helps protect the driver from heavy impacts. Also, the tubes push the engine out the bottom of the car in a crash . . . rather than into the driver's lap! However, they are strong enough that a tap or a bang by the front end of the car will not cause them to collapse too early. An important strength and safety feature of the chassis is a steel "firewall." This heavy piece of metal helps keep the engine's heat from filling up the **cockpit**. Even with the firewall, the temperature around a driver's feet can reach 140 degrees Fahrenheit (60° C) during a race.

The "rear clip" of the chassis surrounds the fuel cell, which is what NASCAR calls the gas tank. This section, too, is designed to collapse quickly in a crash, while remaining strong enough to withstand bumps and slams. The fuel cell (page 22) has its own safety features to keep gasoline from spilling. All of these pieces of the chassis are welded together to form a super-strong steel skeleton. Welding is a way of joining two pieces of metal to make them nearly as strong as one solid piece of metal. Workers use intense heat from a flaming torch to melt the metal pieces together. They also use a metal "glue" that they form between the pieces; when it hardens, the two pieces have become one.

Safety First

The heavy steel of the roll cage plays a huge part in protecting the driver during a crash or collision. However, the COT has other features created for the same reason. The window areas are larger, for instance, making it easier for drivers to climb out.

10

The cockpit itself, the place where the driver sits, is slightly taller and wider to make more room for the drivers. "I absolutely feel safer in this car," says Dale Earnhardt Jr. "This car has a lot of room in it." Also, the chassis of the COT has more steel plating and framing on the sides than earlier cars did. Finally, special materials are used in the door areas of the chassis that help absorb the energy of the crash. A crash during testing proved it to former NASCAR champion Dale Jarrett.

"The car obviously does its job," he said after walking away with no injuries. Even "The King" is impressed. "It's about time," said Richard Petty, who won seven NASCAR titles. "We've been running basically the same car since 1981, and all they've done is refine it [little by little]. The big deal with this new Car of Tomorrow is safety." If the goal of the Car of Tomorrow was to make sure that more drivers reach tomorrow, it seems to have succeeded.

HANS Device

A special safety feature of NASCAR vehicles that started before the COT is the HANS device. The letters stand for "head-and-neck system." Safety experts say that in a crash, a driver's head might whip around dangerously. The HANS device was created to help prevent this. Sadly, it took the tragic death of Dale Earnhardt Sr. to force NASCAR to make it part of every drivers' gear. To use the HANS, drivers slip a collar over their shoulders that is connected to their helmet and to the back of their seat, set inside the roll cage. In a crash, cables will pull tight, helping keep a driver's head and neck from moving suddenly. Some drivers have pointed to the HANS device as a key reason why they were not hurt during a wreck.

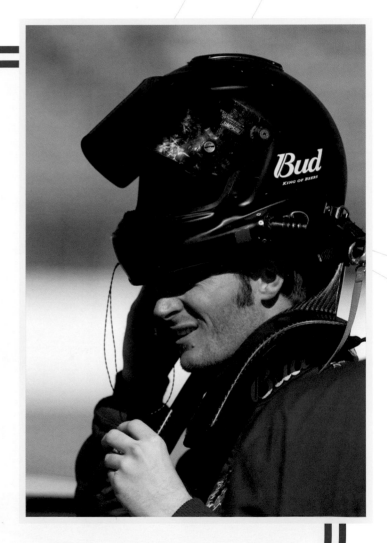

Dale Earnhardt Jr. slips on the collar and brace of the HANS device as he pulls on his racing helmet.

The Body of Work

Forming the body of a NASCAR racecar combines science, art, and a lot of hard work. Before the fancy colors make it onto the body, there are many steps of work to perform. Let's see how a NASCAR car body comes together.

The Outside Shell

With a chassis built, the next step is to form the body of the car. These two main pieces of the machine are created separately and then put together. The body fits over the chassis almost like a glove fits over a hand. The chassis helps create the shape, while the body (or the glove) gets all the attention and color!

The bodies, or shells, of the NASCAR COT are made of steel plates that are carefully cut and welded together. The shape of the car must match exactly to the COT design, though the **sponsoring** carmakers can adjust the front ends of the various team cars to somewhat look like their passenger cars.

The big change from older NASCAR car bodies and the COT is the wing at the rear of the car. It can be adjusted to match a driver's needs.

Before the COT was used in races, it was tested over and over, as shown here.

Designing the COT Body

Creating the shape of the COT body took more than five years of testing and design. As with chassis design, computers were used to try out many different looks for the COT body. They also created clay models of the COT body and put them in **wind tunnels**. These special boxes helped show how air flowed over each part of the shell. Over the design period, the designers started with the basic NASCAR shape, but changed it in many small ways to make it safer and slower. Did we say slower? That's right, one of the aims of the COT is to slow drivers down a bit. Mostly for safety, but it is also to help make races closer and more exciting to watch. A big way that the bodies help slow things down has to do with **aerodynamics**. That's a big word for how

something moves through the air. At the high speeds at which NASCAR drivers race their cars, even a tiny adjustment can play a big part. The biggest part of aerodynamics in NASCAR is called "downforce." The COT is designed to "push" the car down toward the track as it moves through the air. This push helps the drivers maintain control of the car at high speed. Without it, the cars might slip into the walls, especially when turning. Controlling downforce on the COT is done with a "splitter" at the front that can raise or lower, depending on how a driver likes his car. A new rear wing on the top of the trunk section also helps direct air to create downforce.

13

Sparks Flying

Whether making the COT body or one of the older NASCAR shells, the process is one that mixes technology and art. The first step is using **templates** to form the pieces of the body. These templates are put on sheets of steel, which is then cut to match the template exactly. By using these templates over and over again, the makers can be sure that their car is exactly the shape that they want it to be—or, exactly the shape that NASCAR says it should be. In the next step, expert builders called **fabricators** take these pre-cut steel pieces and **rivet** them together to form the body shape.

However, since everything is curved in one way or another, that means bending, rolling, or curving hard steel. They use heavy rollers, small hand tools, or sometimes just strength to form and shape the steel into the body. After all of the pieces are carefully riveted together, they are also welded. In this step, the pieces are firmly put together. But just as importantly, the entire skin is made smooth, with no cracks, bumps, or seams. Remember aerodynamics? One little bump might slow a car down a fraction. And with many NASCAR races decided by inches, that might make a difference.

You can see the sheets of metal used to form the body of the Car of Tomorrow here. This car body will be put over the chassis from page 8.

Putting One and One Together

With the chassis completed and the body smoothed carefully, it's time to put them together. But before that can happen, a few things are installed. First comes the drivers' seat, which is placed inside the roll cage and bolted to the chassis. Each seat is custom molded to fit the car's driver. This means that he'll have a more comfortable place to sit, but it also means that he won't move around much during the rocking ride around the track. The steel seats are not padded like the ones that you ride in, but they do help protect the drivers in crashes. Attached to the seat is a five-point seat belt, or harness. The thick nylon straps go over the driver's shoulders, around his waist, and up between his legs. A quick-release button is over his chest, to let him pop the belts off in case he has to get out quickly. Some of the car's electronics, hoses, and tubes are sometimes installed at this point, when they can be accessed easily. The car is carefully inspected at every stage by the carmakers. Even one loose weld can spell the difference between winning and crashing.

Windows?

The COT, like older NASCAR designs, does not have side windows . . . or doors! Drivers climb in through the window openings, which are then covered by a nylon net during the race. The front and rear windshields are attached to the body. They're not made of glass, however, but of **Lexan**, a super-strong plastic. Over the Lexan, most teams put three or four layers of sticky, clear film. As the race moves on, they just pull off one layer of this film at a time. This is faster and better than trying to clean the plastic with water during the heat of a pit stop.

NASCAR vehicles don't have windows. The black, nylon netting is clipped in place during races to protect drivers from flying debris.

15

Splashes of Color

A racetrack full of silver-painted cars would be boring . . . and confusing! With the basic car built, it's time to get out the paintbrushes and create racing, rolling billboards!

Making it Beautiful

With the body connected to the chassis, there are several more steps to go before the car is ready to hit the racetrack. The next step is to add color! After the shell is welded to be as smooth as possible, a special type of paint called "primer" is sprayed on it inside and out. This helps protect the metal from water and air, which might cause rust. The car's basic color is then painted on. Special artists come in and paint on large logos, the car number, and other major design features. After the paint dries, stickers from various sponsors are applied all over the car. This process can take two to three days and cost as much as $15,000. However, in the last few years, many teams have started using vinyl stickers, or "skins," instead of paint. They can be put on very quickly and cost much less. They are printed with the logos, sponsor names, car number, and more, then carefully applied almost like a skin on the car. Workers smooth the skins on, removing any air bubbles. Some teams use as many as seven separate stickers to cover the entire car. One team used a single skin to decorate its Spider-Man car.

See how many colors you can find in this racing action photo. Teams choose their colors to match their major sponsors, then add stickers for smaller sponsors.

Making It Legal!

Remember that the COT is designed to give every NASCAR team the same type of car to drive in. To make sure that all of the teams show up at the track with that car, NASCAR officials do careful inspections before every race. This can take from four to ten hours. The first step is using NASCAR's own templates to make sure that the body is exactly the right shape. Differences of fractions of an inch can cause a team to fail its inspection. The cars are weighed to make sure they hit NASCAR minimums of 3,400 pounds (1,545 kg) without the driver. The engines, safety features, fuel cells, and undersides are also inspected carefully to make sure that no one is trying anything funny. After practice or qualifying runs, and before the main race, the cars are often inspected again to make sure that nothing sneaky is going on!

Like cars waiting at the local gas pump, NASCAR racers line up for prerace inspection.

Something Funny

Why all the inspections? While it would be nice to think that everyone plays by the rules and never does anything illegal, it's not always that way. Over the decades, drivers and teams have come up with hundreds of ways to squeeze around the rules, all in an effort to gain more speed for their cars. In 2006, Michael Waltrip was docked points in the standings when his team added something illegal to its fuel mixture. In 2007, Jeff Gordon and Jimmie Johnson (who have six NASCAR titles between them) were each penalized 100 points and fined after inspectors found a few things "funny" about their fenders and other car parts. The COT and the inspections are designed to make it harder and harder for teams to cheat.

Under the Car

Beneath the chassis, beneath the shell, even behind the tires, are several very important parts of the COT. How do drivers steer . . . and how do they stop? Let's find out.

Keeping It Straight

By now the car has a skeleton—the chassis—and a body, but what about its arms and legs? On a car, you might say that the axles and wheels are its limbs. The axle is the long, metal pole that connects the wheels on opposite sides of the car. The tires are attached to the outside of the wheels at the ends of the axles. The front wheels are attached to the steering assembly, and tires are attached to the wheels with five **lug nuts**.

On tight-turning road courses like this one at Sonoma, Jeff Gordon and other drivers sometimes find themselves partly airborne.

Suspension Systems

Along with the axles, it's time to put in the **suspension**. When your car goes over a bump in the road, do you feel your car rock up and down a bit? The COT, like your car, has parts that help it absorb, or take in, these bumps. During a high-speed race over a track that gets bumpier and bumpier as the cars go around, a NASCAR driver's suspension is very important. Many drivers and crew members feel that the suspension, which affects how a car handles, is almost as important as the engine in making a car go as fast as it can go. The suspension on the COT includes shock absorbers and springs on all four wheels, as well as parts that can be adjusted by the **pit crew** during a race (see box on p. 19). The idea is to create a "ride" that makes the car go as fast as possible.

Under each tire is this disk that contains the brake (silver panel) and lugs, which are the five bolts (count 'em!) that hold the tire to the car.

Tight vs. Loose

Fans watching NASCAR on TV will often hear the announcers or drivers talk about the car being "**tight**" or "**loose**." What they are talking about is how the car is handling, or steering. Tight means that the car won't turn well in corners. Instead of going into the curve, the front of the car is felt to slide away from the turn, toward the outside wall. If a car is loose, it feels like the back end is doing the same thing; that is, it feels to the driver as if the back wants to head toward the wall instead of through the turn. During a pit stop, the springs on each wheel can be slightly adjusted to help correct these problems. Pit crew members can use a wrench to quickly "tighten" or "loosen" the springs.

Somebody "got loose" here! Losing control of a "loose" car can often lead to wrecks like this one at Bristol Motor Speedway.

Stop That Car!

The steering makes the car go straight, while the suspension helps keep it steady. What makes the car stop? Now we're talking about brakes. The small silver panel on the outside of the wheels in the picture on page 18 is part of one of the four large "disc" brakes on the typical NASCAR car. When the driver pushes down on the brake pedal at his feet, these panels, or pads, press onto the wheel, slowing and stopping it from turning. Since these cars are running at such high speeds, the brakes have to be very strong. You'll often see smoke coming from under the car when a driver has to stop very suddenly, such as when he's trying to avoid a wreck or stop his spinning car. Brakes can also be changed from track to track. At large superspeedways, brakes aren't used much and can be lighter and smaller. On twisty road courses where braking is often and sudden, teams install more powerful brakes. The brakes used in NASCAR races are changed after every race because of wear and tear. When you are going nearly 200 miles per hour (321.9 km/h), you need great brakes!

19

Making It Go . . . Fast!

The COT has its chassis, body, suspension, and tires. Now, what does it need to get moving? The massive NASCAR engine, of course. Let's pop the hood and see what's growling underneath!

The Power Under the Hood

The average passenger car puts out about 200 **horsepower** and is about 120 to 180 cubic inches (1966.4 to 2949.7 cm³) in basic size. Under the hood of a powerful NASCAR racer, however, is a gigantic 358 cubic-inch (5866.6 cm³) V-8 that can put out 850 horsepower! (Why horsepower? That term was first used when car engines were developed in the late 1800s. At the time, the standard of power was the horse, so builders compared their "newfangled" products to how many horses the engine would replace!) The powerful NASCAR engine can rocket the COT to speeds of more than 200 miles (321.9 km) per hour in the long straightaways of superspeedways. And thanks to the fact that they don't have mufflers, NASCAR engines make a lot of noise! The V-8 means that the engine has eight **cylinders**. Basically, a car engine works when a gasoline-air mixture fires in a cylinder, which pushes a piston, which turns a driveshaft to the wheels. Those pistons can work so hard and so fast that the driveshaft (the long pole that connects the engine to the rear wheels) might turn as many as 9,000 times per minute! That measurement, revolutions per minute, or RPM, is one that you might hear during a race. Every racing team in NASCAR works with one carmaker that is responsible for supplying the basic engine parts to the team. Those parts include the main engine block, the heads that cover the pistons, and other key parts. Beyond that, each team puts its own engines together based on its driving style, expertise, and budget.

Don't worry, this crew member will get out before the race starts! Race team crews often have to switch engines several times during a race weekend.

Rules, Rules, Rules

NASCAR, of course, keeps a very close eye on what teams do to the engines. They inspect the engines before and after races to make sure that all rules are followed. They check to make sure that all parts are legal and that teams have not changed the basic engine parts supplied by the carmakers. NASCAR also checks where the engine is mounted. It can't be too far forward or too low, which might give the car a speed advantage. Still, with all of these inspections, teams are always looking for that one little edge that can put them one step closer to the finish line than the other guys! But if a team is caught breaking the rules, officials might penalize them by taking away points or even laps run.

Keeping Cool

These engines are so powerful that they also get very, very hot during races. A big part of the crew's work before and during the race is to make sure that the engines don't overheat. The main system to cool the engine is an oil-and-water mix that runs through tubes in and around the engine. Oil also circulates around the pistons to keep them lubricated, or moving smoothly. A radiator in the engine cools the oil so that it can cool the engine parts as it circulates. Air also helps cool the engine, rushing in through a grill at the front of the car. Crews have to make sure that this grill stays clean during a race. Even a loose piece of paper covering the grill can have a disastrous effect on a hot engine.

This head-on shot of a typical NASCAR V-8 shows the many belts and hoses that help keep its various parts turning and moving.

A Truck Full of Engines

NASCAR teams bring one or two cars to each race, but they might bring four or five complete engines. These cars, engines, and all of the parts and tools needed to fix them, travel in gigantic 18-wheel trucks called "haulers." These haulers are like complete garages on wheels. With the gear carried on the haulers, race crews can rebuild their cars and engines almost from the ground up on-site at the track. Engines are the parts that are most often changed. Before each race, drivers have to run qualifying laps to set their places in the starting order. For these few laps, teams make up special engines that are made with lighter parts. Those parts wouldn't stand up to a full race, but can last a few laps. And those few pounds of difference might make a car go just fast enough to earn a high starting spot. Teams also create engines to use while working on the car's set up during practice laps. This lighter, less-powerful engine won't last long, either, but then again…it doesn't have to. Finally, they have one engine that is "dialed in" for full-time racing use. This uses the sturdiest parts and hoses. "Dialed in" is a term that drivers use for getting their cars ready to race. Crews adjust everything from tire pressure to fuel mixture to the height of the rear wings. After every race, the engines are almost completely taken apart. Worn parts are replaced, and all parts are cleaned and lubricated before being replaced. It's worth the effort—a new engine can cost more than $75,000! That's one reason that team owners work so hard to get and keep sponsors—this is an expensive sport!

Race crews can work on the engines right up until the race starts, as Matt Kenseth's team is doing here.

During a pit stop, a crew member pours fuel out of this can into the fuel cell, located in the back of the car.

Gassing Up

Making this powerful engine go is special gasoline, provided by NASCAR to all of the teams to ensure fairness. The new COT car can hold about 18 gallons (68.1 L), a bit less than the 22 gallons (83.3 L) in previous NASCAR vehicles. The gas is held in a fuel cell at the back of the COT. To prevent dangerous spills of gasoline during crashes, the fuel cell is specially made from several layers. The layers include a steel box, a foam substance that will compress upon impact, and a thick, plastic container called a "bladder" that actually holds the gasoline. During a pit stop, crew members can empty two nine-gallon gas cans into the car in less than 10 seconds! Try that next time your family car stops for gas!

Restrictor Plate Racing

During the 1980s, as cars got faster and faster, NASCAR realized that it had to slow down the massive machines, especially on superspeedways with their high **banking**. The all-time NASCAR speed record of more than 212 miles (341 km) per hour was set in 1987 by Bill Elliott at superspeedway Talladega. To slow things, NASCAR introduced the **restrictor plate**. This flat piece of metal, with four holes in it, is bolted to the top of the engine for races at superspeedways. The holes reduce the amount of air that goes into the engine. Since the engine runs when air and the gasoline combine to make a series of small explosions, the less air, the smaller the explosions, and the slower the car.

Rubber to the Road

If everything goes right during a race, the only parts of the car to touch the track are four that we have not discussed yet. Now it's time to put the hammer down and talk tires!

Not Just Everyday Tires

Your family car probably needs new tires about every 40,000 miles (64,374 km) or so. While driving a NASCAR COT, a driver might need to change his tires every 100 miles (160 km) . . . and sometimes more often than that! On a racing weekend, a team might use 14 or 15 sets of tires. They also cost more, about $400 each as compared to about $100 each for the family car. The treads are 11.5 inches (29 cm) wide, about two inches (5 cm) wider than on a typical passenger car tire. Your family car's tires are filled with air (oxygen and carbon dioxide), but COT tires use nitrogen. And have you seen the treads on your tires? They have grooves in the rubber to help grip the road and let water roll through them. NASCAR COT tires have no tread at all; they have smooth rubber surfaces with no marks or grooves at all. That's why in wet weather NASCAR races are stopped. The tires are not made to run through water of any kind. However, the smooth tire surface is perfect for the high-speed turning that NASCAR racers do; it "grips" the track.

Each NASCAR team is supplied with the same type of tires by the Goodyear company. This ensures that one team doesn't have an unfair advantage.

 **24**

After warm-ups, tires are tested for wear by crew members. Knowing how tires wear on each track helps a crew decide when it's time to change tires during a race.

Working on Tires

Most teams have several crew members whose only job is to take care of tires. After a team gets the tires from NASCAR, these crew members carefully check them, measure them, and inflate them as determined by the crew chief and driver. The tires are labeled "R" or "L" for right or left. Tires on a car's left side wear out faster, as the shape of most tracks means that more weight is on them as the car turns left over and over. After a practice run, the tires are carefully measured again. Special tools (left) show how much wear the tread has gone through. Crew members can also look for wear markers built into the tires. These are small metal knobs built into the layers of rubber of the tire itself. As the rubber wears away during the hot practice laps around the track, the metal is exposed. Measuring how much metal shows through can tell crew members how much wear the tires went through. They can then make adjustments to the pressure of the gas inside the tires. Some tires might be used again (they're called "scuffs") and they are cleaned with a blowtorch to remove the bits of rubber and track that stick to them. When a driver is going full speed, the only things between him and the road are those four tires. At high speed, a section of rubber about one hand wide is touching the road at any one time. That's a lot of pressure to put on an inch of rubber. Every team takes great care with its tires!

The Old Tire Days

Today's NASCAR teams have the benefit of an air gun to change tires. These tools use air pressure to loosen or tighten the five lug nuts in just seconds. But before air guns, teams relied on good old wrenches. The classic tire wrench came in the form of an X with a wrench at each of its four ends. The tire changer put a wrench on a lug nut and spun the X hard!

Different Track, Different Tire

Different types of tires are used at most types of tracks, with the changes including the type or thickness of rubber or the tread thickness. NASCAR keeps careful records of which types work best on the concrete, asphalt, or mixed surfaces. In fact, they use 18 different types of tire surfaces! Also, special tires are used on tracks that are one mile (1.6 km) or more in length. These tires have a special inner liner that is almost like a second tire. When there is a blowout on one of these tires, this inner layer helps the driver keep control of the car long enough to return to the pits. Why these tracks only? Because the higher speeds and greater wear on the tires at these longer tracks are more likely to cause damage. And blowing a tire at 200 miles (321.9 km) per hour can be very dangerous!

Attaching Tires

How are the tires attached to the wheels? They're attached with five lug nuts. To make changing them easier, the nuts are attached to the tires before the race with a glue-like substance. Then the tire changers (see box at right) just tighten the nuts quickly. The lug nuts on NASCAR vehicles are different than on your car in this way: to prevent them from sticking or mis-threading in the heat of a race, they have half as much threading (the spiral parts inside the nut itself).

During a pit stop, the jack man (far left) lifts the car to let the tire carriers work. In the center of the picture, that's a tire carrier bouncing a used tire back to the pit wall!

Tire Guys

During a pit stop, five crew members are dedicated to changing tires. Here are their jobs, which they can complete in as little as 15 seconds!

Jack man: Lifts the right side (and then the left) side of the car using a large aluminum jack.

Front and rear tire carriers: Lift the new tire over the pit wall and bring it into position by the front or rear wheels, first on the right side and then on the left. They also bring the used tires back to the pit wall.

Front and rear tire changers: Using an air gun, they loosen the five lug nuts on the right wheels and then tighten the lug nuts on the new tires. Then they repeat the process on the left tires.

Look directly under the number 43 to see where the jack man has placed his tool. With just one push, he will be able to raise the tires on one side off the ground.

The Ones That Get Away

Pit crews lugging heavy tires while working at top speed sometimes make mistakes. There is nothing that a tire changer wants to see less than one of his tires slipping from his grasp and bouncing down pit road! In fact, if that does happen, the driver and his car can be hit with a penalty of time or a return to the pits on the next lap, which can sometimes hurt their chances for winning. At a race in Las Vegas in 2007, Jimmie Johnson's crew let a tire bounce away and he had to "pass through" the pits one more time. He still managed to win the race, however. In fact, he came back to win the NASCAR Nextel Cup that year with a four-win streak late in the season. At another race, a NASCAR official who was monitoring Johnson's team saved the day by snagging a bouncing tire before it could get in the way of other cars. At the 1999 Daytona 500, a runaway tire bounced away from one team for several hundred feet before it could be grabbed. Other cars heading in for pit stops were roaring down pit road and had to swerve to avoid it. However, with pit crews now training full-time like athletes, such mistakes are rare.

What You See

By now, the COT is just about ready for the road, so let's wrap up our tour of the car with a few more important items.

Pick a Number

Everybody knows which driver is in which car. They've got the car numbers memorized like NFL fans know that Peyton Manning is No. 18. Car numbers in NASCAR go from 0 to 99, but also include 01, 02, 03, etc. NASCAR itself owns all of the car numbers, but assigns them to team owners. The team owners then choose which drivers get which cars. Once a driver gets a number, however, it becomes a big part of his

Thank you, thank you! These stickers are what a sponsor gets for providing money to a racing team. The large number identifies the driver.

identity. A problem can come up when drivers switch teams. In 2008, Dale Earnhardt Jr. started racing for Rick Hendrick's team. Problem was, Dale Jr.'s famous No. 8 car was controlled by his old team, DEI Racing, which was run by his stepmother Teresa. So the man who wrote a best-selling book called *Driver #8* would no longer be Driver 8. Instead, he became No. 88. The large number is painted or stickered onto the sides and top of the car so that fans on TV and in the stands can easily find their favorites. Near the numbers on the side are dozens of sponsor stickers, too.

Bump on Top

On the top of the COT, you'll probably see a small disk of metal. This disk helps the driver communicate with his crew back in the pits. It's called a "transponder," and sends it signals on car performance via radio to the crew. The crew chief can monitor various parts of the car's systems and let the driver and his crew know if there is anything wrong. This information is also partly made available to television viewers. The transponder lets TV directors use all sorts of cool graphics that identify the cars for TV viewers.

Fans know from this signature that Dale Earnhardt Jr. is behind the wheel of this car.

You might also see the tiny camera that is sometimes placed inside the front windshield so that fans watching at home on TV get a unique, high-speed, driver's-eye view of the action.

Lights Off!

Looking at the front of a NASCAR COT, you might think that they have headlights. Guess again . . . those aren't real lights, but stickers. When races are held at night, the track is lit brightly enough that headlights are not needed. The "lights" that you see are really just stickers to make the cars look more like regular cars instead of racing machines.

Jeff Gordon's number 24 car looks like it would work well at night, but those lights are fake!

Driver's View

The final stop on our tour of the COT is the dashboard. Drivers are strapped into their specially designed seats, and they buckle their five-point harness. Then they attach the steering wheel. The wheel is removed when drivers climb in and out to make the climb easier for them. Once the drivers are strapped in, they look down at a set of switches, dials, and gear levers. The dials keep track of battery power, oil pressure, and engine performance. There is no gas gauge as in a passenger car, nor do they have a speedometer. The dials in the NASCAR vehicles are each turned so that when the arrow in the dial is pointing to the proper number, the arrow will be straight up. That way, drivers can just look for up-and-down arrows in a quick glance instead of having to read numbers while driving inches away from another car at 150 miles (241 km) per hour! Switches on the dashboard control **ignition**, battery power, an oil pump, and other parts of the engine. Drivers usually only have to use them to get started and rarely during a race. The gearshift lever is very close to the right side of the steering wheel, and is much smaller and shorter than most types seen in passenger cars. At the top of the front window is a rearview mirror that stretches across the whole car, giving the driver a complete view behind and to the side of him. For safety reasons, there are no sideview mirrors on NASCAR racers.

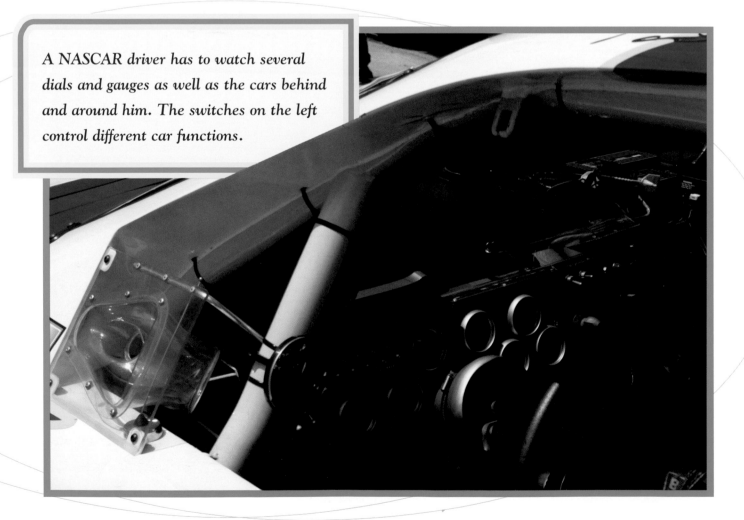

A NASCAR driver has to watch several dials and gauges as well as the cars behind and around him. The switches on the left control different car functions.

Pulling It All Together

So now the COT is ready to race. The car has gone from a diagram on a computer to a steel skeleton. The body went from a clay model in a wind tunnel to a sleek, colorful racing machine. The body shell was decorated with the colors of the rainbow and the logos of all-important sponsors. Into this bright shell, the teams put one of the most powerful engines in the world, mighty enough to pull this heavy car nearly 200 miles (321.9 km) per hour. That engine needs to run superhot for four hours, but the car will roll on tires made to last only about an hour. The teams also added suspension systems dialed in to be perfect to within a fraction of an inch. Controlling this machine is the driver, who is strapped into a place that has been made as safe as technology can make it. He and his crew

Before a NASCAR race, teams scramble in the garage and pit area to fine-tune their cars.

will have "dialed in" the car to perfectly match his driving skills and the particular track that they'll race on that weekend. The engine is tuned over and over to be able to survive three or more hours of high-heat, high-energy action. He climbs in through the window, straps on his HANS device and five-point seating harness, and makes sure his helmet radio is working. Meanwhile, off the track, dozens of crew members get ready to deal with any emergency. Finally, like the other 42 cars that will start this NASCAR race, the only thing left is for that driver to push the starter . . . and head out to the track to make the car do what it does best—go really, really fast!

Glossary

aerodynamics   The science of air moving over an object

axle   A long bar on which wheels turn

banking   At racetracks, the angle or tilt of the roadway in the corners of the track

chassis   The steel "skeleton" of a car

cockpit   The place where the driver sits

cylinder   A chamber, or tube, within which a piston, or disk, pumps up and down

fabricator   A person who shapes sheet steel into a NASCAR car body

horsepower   A measurement of an engine's power

ignition   A system that provides a spark, causing the fuel-air mixture in an internal combustion engine to combust, or ignite

loose   In racing, a term that means that a car's back end wants to drift to the outside of the track

lug nuts   The five metal objects that are used to connect a tire to a car

pit crew   Race team members who change the car's tires and refuel it when the driver stops the car during a "pit stop"

rivet   To fasten or secure firmly with a metal bolt

sponsor   A company that gives money to a person or team in exchange for promotion of the company's products or services

stock car   An automobile made in a factory and available for purchase by the general public

suspension   The parts of a car that help it handle bumps, turns, and rough roads

template   A piece of metal used as a pattern for other pieces

tight   In racing, a term that means that a car's front end wants to drift to the outside of the track

wind tunnel   A room in which air is pushed over objects at high speed to see how the air moves over those objects

Index